From
RAGS
to
RICHES

*How We Made Our Christian Marriage
and Businesses a Success*

Joseph *and* **Annette Trawick**

FROM RAGS TO RICHES
HOW WE MADE OUR CHRISTIAN MARRIAGE AND BUSINESSES A SUCCESS

iUniverse books may be ordered through booksellers or by contacting:

iUniverse
1663 Liberty Drive
Bloomington, IN 47403
www.iuniverse.com
844-349-9409

ISBN: 978-1-6632-2253-4 (sc)
ISBN: 978-1-6632-2252-7 (hc)
ISBN: 978-1-6632-2255-8 (e)

Library of Congress Control Number: 2021911621

Print information available on the last page.

iUniverse rev. date: 06/08/2021

To our Lord Jesus Christ, who is the first person in our lives. Without him, our success in life would not be possible.

To our deceased parents, for whom we hold great admiration and love.

To our children and grandchildren, we love you, and we appreciate the joy that all of you have brought to our lives.

To our friends and community that were there for us, even when they thought we did not feel their presence. Your prayers, love, and support never went unnoticed, and we are forever thankful to all of you.

Contents

Introduction

What do you want out of life? What kind of mate do you want? What kind of career or job and marriage are you seeking?

Is it the right one? Is it the wrong one? Do you want the same thing in life that your mate wants? Or are you so different that you cannot stand the sight of each other?

Some people choose mates because of their families or for financial reasons or popularity, but choosing a person for the wrong reason can be disastrous. When you choose your mate, let it be your choice—because of your inner feelings, your gut feelings, and your "mother wit." (In this book, *mother wit* refers to common sense.)

Do not let anyone else make that final decision for you. You know what you want and how you want it. You know when you want it and where you want it.

That's you. The decisions you make are decisions you will have to live with throughout your lifetime. Be honest with yourself and dig deeply into your heart, especially when choosing someone with whom you plan to live the rest of your life.

We are all God's children. He gave us all the ability to be and do whatever we set out to become and do. We all have faults and shortcomings, but God gave us the ability and know-how to deal with those issues. We are all human beings and make mistakes. Our first priority should be to recognize that we have made a mistake, and the second should be to correct the mistake.

It's how you deal with and correct your mistakes that will make or break you. Then, you can move on with your life.

Making a career with your chosen mate is also a challenge. You will have up-and-down disagreements on different things, but you can shake it up and pour it out as one decision on which you both can agree. That's progress!

Some people choose jobs or careers based on the salary, instead of for the pleasure and enjoyment of that job or career. Choosing a job is similar to choosing a mate—you should love what you do and enjoy the outcome. If you are not happy, move on.

We are going to take you down a path of the good and the ugly— the struggles we faced in keeping our marriage together and how we made our Christian marriage and businesses a success.

I (Annette) dropped out of high school due to pregnancy; I completed the ninth grade. As I traveled the road of adulthood and pursued my dream to become a nurse, I was determined not to be poor anymore.

I was born into a family of ten: my two parents, three sisters, and four brothers. Ours was a dysfunctional family, and we had to strive to survive. My mother carried a very large part of the burden of support for the family, and my father did the best he could.

During my childhood, I knew I had to do something to live a better life. I never went back to school but did obtain my GED and got a job so I could take care of my son and help my parents.

I moved to Atlanta, Georgia, to go to school for my LPN (licensed practical nurse) certification because I didn't have appropriate transportation in the rural area where I lived. I left my son in the care of my mother, and I would send money home to her every week to help her.

I found God in my life when I was a little girl. It seemed as if everything that I set out to do was successful. I would always say, "I am a child of God, and I was put here for a reason." I believed in prayer and God.

My mother, Bertha Mae Hogans Todd, made sure that we went to church every Sunday. We walked through the woods for five miles to get to church.

I said my prayer every night before I went to bed: "Now I lay me down to sleep. I pray the Lord my soul to keep. If I should die before I wake, I pray the Lord my soul to take."

I always loved to be around the elderly; there was something about them that I enjoyed. My mother always taught me to treat people right, especially my elders.

I put my trust in the Lord Jesus Christ and was able to complete my LPN program, as well as earning my RN (registered nurse) license, and attending the Medical College of Georgia, where I earned a master's degree as a clinical nurse specialist in gerontology.

I later married but was a widow at age forty-six, when I met Joseph. I was lonely, troubled, and confused. I had a good education and was financially stable, but there was a void in my life.

Sitting alone one night, looking up in the ceiling, I asked the Lord, "Why am I alone and so unhappy? I have a good job that I love, four handsome sons, friends and family, financial stability, and a brand-new car in the garage." But something was missing.

Even so, I had a feeling deep inside that I could not explain. It was a feeling of comfort and relaxation, as if I was held in someone's arms and was being comforted, but I could not see that person. One day, my godfather was standing beneath my bedroom window, and I shared my feelings of loneliness with him.

He told me, "Don't worry. God will send somebody to you."

And he did! God is good. That person was my husband, Joseph.

Joseph and I were married, but our marriage was attacked by many obstacles. We held each other's hands, prayed, locked the outsiders out of our lives, and stayed focused. We knew we loved each other, and we refused to allow our marriage to be destroyed.

Outsiders made many attempts to turn our children against us and to ruin our marriage. With God in our lives, we were determined not to allow the devil to come between us and our children. We stayed closed to our children and had many prayer sessions together.

We gave honor to the first person in our lives, the Lord Jesus Christ. We put all our faith in him and knew, as we walked our path, that our Lord Jesus Christ led the way. As the late Roy Trawick Sr. once said, "What God put together, no man can separate."

Joseph and I started several businesses together. One successful business was the Certified Nurse Assistant Training Program. It has been promoted as one of the most successful programs in Georgia.

Joseph is the CEO of Global Transit, LLC, which is a successful transportation program that transports individuals to and from medical appointments.

When we started these businesses, we had our ups and downs There were times when we didn't know if we could make payroll or pay the utility bills and/or the mortgage. It was devastating to think what our employees would say about us and the company, after they'd worked for two weeks but didn't get a paycheck.

Now, Joseph will share his journey of walking with the Lord.

I (Joseph) had been divorced for twenty-three years before Annette and I met. I often shared with her that I had spent many years alone, unhappy, with emptiness in my life, until one day, I discovered the Lord. I had been along many dark paths throughout my lifetime.

I finished high school and always wanted to own my own business. I had a history of not having longevity on any job because of my lack of inner strength to take directions from others. I wanted to be the boss.

I want to share my discovery of the Lord Jesus Christ as an inner feeling. I didn't know what was going on, but I knew that when I went into a hole or was met with an obstacle, I was able to overcome it.

Sometimes my heart was so heavy; I was burdened and worried over what I should do. I wasn't able to pay my bills. There was no food in the refrigerator. I didn't even have enough gas to get to work the next day.

I went into my quiet bedroom; the only light was from an over-the-bed lamp. I read the Bible and recited Bible verse after Bible verse, and I asked the Lord why I was having so much bad luck.

After I read seven or eight pages of the Bible, I experienced a warm, peculiar feeling. The feeling was just like a breath of fresh air coming down inside my body. I felt I was being cleansed and that all my worries, aches, and pains were fading away. It was one of the best feelings that I've had ever had in my life. I didn't feel alone anymore, and when I walked, I felt the Lord right there with me.

Annette and I would like you to walk with us and the Lord as we share our struggles and relate how we made our Christian marriage and businesses a success.

Chapter 1

Annette: Growing Up Poor

As a little girl, wandering up and down the path from my home to the neighbor's home, I would look at what they had and thought it would be so nice to have those things such as a radio to listen to music and to listen to stories as if they were happening right in front of me. Back then, in 1960, we didn't have television, but we could listen to the radio stories, like "Br'er Rabbit," "Red Wolf," and "The Little House on the Hill."

I grew up in Irwinton, a small town in Wilkinson County, Georgia. The town was small, but the people there had big hearts full of love. We all knew each other and would look out for one another and offer a helping hand, even if it wasn't needed.

I contributed my skills, knowledge, love of God, and strong family values to my family, friends, and the Wilkinson County community at large. It is because of them that I'm able to sit here today and reflect. I will always cherish their support for me throughout all of my endeavors.

Our home was not the best, but it was livable— there were areas in the house that kept my feet from touching the sand and areas that kept the rain off my head. The wooden stove in the corner kept us warm when we had enough wood to keep the fire burning. But that was OK too because we had love in the home—and we had each other to keep our feet warm. Sharing the bed with my younger sister was an advantage in the winter. Sometimes, lying in bed at night and being able to look through the ceiling and see the stars or clouds was an advantage too, especially in the summer. At least it wasn't so hot, for we didn't have an air-conditioner to keep us cool. It was when the rain came that I wished for more shelter.

I will never forget the time that I was walking in the front room and fell through a crack in the floor. I sustained a deep cut to my left thigh. My parents were unable to get me to a doctor, so my mother provided the best care that she could so that I did not bleed to death. The scar from that accident remains visible to this day.

When I started school, I had to walk there. It didn't matter if there was rain, sleet, or snow, my siblings and I had to go. My mother believed in our getting a good education. She was smart too.

I sometimes walked without shoes or in shoes that were too small, too big, or had holes in them. It didn't matter if I had shoes or not. It didn't matter if I had no sweater or coat in the cold or if my dress was too small or too large, I wore whatever was given to me. The kids on the school bus would laugh at us as they passed by or throw paper balls from the window.

With all that, I still look back on my past and say, "Thank you, Jesus. You brought me a mighty long way." Some of those same kids who would throw paper balls at me and laugh at me as I walked to school are now asking me for a job. And you know what? If I can hire them, I will. God is good. He made it possible so I could.

I am no longer barefoot; I have more shoes than I ever could have imagined. I have more clothes than I ever will be able to wear. And I have more cars than I ever will be able to drive. It's God's work. Thank you!

As I walked to school every day, I read, and when I couldn't read, I sang. I got my education. My God blessed me.

I hated for Christmas to come because I had to play make-believe—I'd lie about what Santa Claus brought me for Christmas. Many times, I got no gift at all, or it was a hand-me-down from others.

Even as an adult, I still have flashbacks of going back to school after Christmas. The teacher would have the students stand in front of the class and tell what they got for Christmas. That was devastating to me. I hated when it was my turn to share, but it was my make-believe moment—or better yet, my wish list after Christmas.

Today, when I talk with professional staff and teachers, I share my experience with them, hoping they won't make their students go through what I had to go through at Christmastime.

To compensate and make myself feel better, I have bought gifts for the needy, especially at Christmas.

Chapter 2

Annette: A Mother's Child

Looking across the highway and into the fields, as far as I can see, there are rows and rows of whiteness. Such memories that brings.

I would awaken at four o'clock in the morning.

"Get up, get up! The bus will be here soon." Off to the cotton field we would go. I was the oldest of my siblings who were still at home with my parents. My older brothers had gone off to the war or had moved out of state to find jobs. My oldest sister had married and moved to Atlanta.

My mother was dependent mainly on me to help her provide for the family. My father was in the home, but his function was one that I will not discuss.

When I reminisce about those days, I remember that I enjoyed being with my mother. I felt a sense of security when I was with her. I also felt that she wanted me by her side and had the same feelings as I did.

Working in the cotton fields was not the only adventure my mom and I had together. We also pulled stumps, picked peaches and vegetables, and sometimes we even made it to the watermelon field. I loved my mother so much, and I enjoyed being with her. A good work ethic was one of my mother's traits. She worked hard to support the family, and no job was too low or too hard for her to handle.

My friends and family tell me now that I am a hard worker and work all the time. I tell them, "I learned from the best." My mom would tell me all the time, "It may seem hard and unfair now, but the end results will be good." I didn't understand what she meant then. The only things that I saw as a result were the calluses on my hands and on the bottoms of my feet.

Now, it rings in my head: hard work will pay off one day. I can honestly say that hard work has paid off for me. I am now sixty-five years old and have not applied for Social Security. I own three businesses with my husband, and I love to work. I get up at five o'clock in the morning four or five times a week to get to the office by eight. It's a joy to me, rather than a challenge.

I attribute my energy and drive to my mother.

At a younger age, I joined the Fountain Grove AME Church in McIntyre, Georgia, along with my siblings.

My mother believed in the Lord, and she taught me to believe in and worship the Lord. She would get my siblings and me up on Sunday mornings, and we would walk about five miles through the woods, down a narrow path, to Sunday school and church. We loved going to this church because our grandmother was one of the founders and the mother of the church.

My biggest fear was stepping on lizards and snakes as we walked. I saw many and often fell as I was running from them. I still have that fear today.

On many Sundays, we did not have nice dresses or shoes like the other children in church, but I felt as rich as they did, sitting next to my mother.

I could talk about my growing-up years all day long, but it brings tears to my eyes when I tumble upon painful memories. I will tell you what really happened in my life when I was age fifteen, and I dropped out of school because I was pregnant.

I really didn't have a childhood because I worked all the time, and after I dropped out of school in the ninth grade, I never went back; instead, I went to work. I worked in my uncle's club. I worked in the peach fields. I picked cotton. I worked wherever I had to work in order to survive. I was so tired of being poor. To make things worse, deep inside of me, I wanted to get pregnant and drop out of school so that I could get a job and help my mom. I often think of this, and when these thoughts come to me, I feel guilty and try to reflect. I wonder if this was my destiny.

When I told my mom that I was pregnant, she didn't scold me or say anything to make me feel ashamed. Her biggest concern was protecting me from my father. I can hear her now, saying, "Joe, leave that girl alone."

Who would think that anyone would come to a good ending by getting pregnant and dropping out of school? I'm still debating that one because I didn't go back to school at age fifteen. Later on, though, I got my GED and then attended college and completed my master's degree.

I call this the work of the Lord. My God is a good God.

And I loved and miss my mom so much.

Chapter 3

Annette: A School Dropout

I am not proud that I dropped out of school, but it did bring me one handsome and intelligent young man and four grandchildren. As I've mentioned, I still have flashbacks of getting pregnant and feeling it was my destiny, a way to get out of poverty. Or maybe it was my signal to get away from a dysfunctional family and to help my mom. I only know that I never looked back. I had a dream and a goal. I wanted to be a nurse.

At age sixteen, I joined the Neighborhood Youth Program for school dropouts. This allowed me to work while going to school to obtain my GED. I completed the program at age seventeen but then learned that I could not take the GED test until I turned eighteen. I falsified my birth certificate and raised my age to eighteen, allowing me to take the test.

I moved to Atlanta to work and go back to school for my LPN certification, while my mom raised my son. I sent her money every week for caring for him. I obtained my LPN and returned home, now with an advanced education.

My first handsome son is now a district manager of a grocery exchange, and I am so proud of him. He has lightened my heart with four beautiful grandkids.

My second handsome son owns his own business, a trucking company. He is a very strong-minded individual, and I feel that he inherited that trait from me. He has rewarded me with four beautiful grandkids.

My mother was so proud of me. I could see it in her eyes. She would tell everyone, "My Faye is a nurse." I was the only child in my family to go off to school and then college and earn an advanced degree. She told me often how proud she was of me. Hard work pays off.

Being a high school dropout but still wanting to go to college was not an easy task. It was difficult. I stayed up late on many nights, reading and studying, over and over again. I would look up words that I didn't understand or couldn't pronounce.

My friends would come by, wanting me to go out to a nightclub with them, but I couldn't go because I had to study. Not only did I have to study, but I also had to work. I worked two jobs while I went to school, and at times it was too much for me to handle, but I knew what I wanted. I knew what I needed to do to get it. I made sacrifices to reach my goals.

I worked from 11:00 p.m. until 7:00 a.m., and I brought my school books to work with me. Numerous times, when I was on my break, I'd fall asleep on the commode with my book in my hands. I was never caught so I maintained my job.

When I was working two jobs, I would finish work and then drive to Athens, Georgia, to attend college classes. By the time I reached campus, the only thing I could remember was getting in the car in Macon, Georgia, going through Eatonton, and ending up in Athens. I could not remember how I got there or going through the other small towns to get to campus.

I knew that it had to be God looking after me and guiding me on that highway. He was there with me. I know that now.

I married at age twenty-five and had two more handsome sons. Son number three has beautiful eyes. He is an over-the-road truck driver and owns his own trucking company as well.

Son number four is my baby. He is a police chief in Irwinton, Georgia. He always wanted to be in law enforcement. When he was age twenty, he had completed the police academy but was not old enough to purchase a gun. My husband had to purchase the gun for him so that he could complete his training. He also owns his own trucking business. From this son, I have four additional grandchildren.

My dropping out of school is not a period of my life that I want to brag about. It's a time I look back on and wonder, *Why couldn't I have done better?* Was that really my way of getting out of poverty, or was getting pregnant a scapegoat method for me?

Age fifteen and pregnant: what disgrace did I bring to my family? As I mentioned, my mom never scolded or shamed me. She was always there and spread her wings to comfort me. My father was a different story. He called me names, belittled me, and chased me in an attempt to whip me. My mom would tell him to leave me alone.

I slept under the neighbor's house for safety—not once but many times—to avoid whippings for reasons I did not understand.

Through all of this, I still loved him as my father.

As I grew older, and others heard about me being a school dropout but then completing college with no other educational background than six months in an after-school program, I was called upon to do motivational speaking.

I went to schools, activity centers, churches, and special events to speak about my life and how I was able to obtain a college degree. I did not enjoy this because I had problems telling the students to stay in school.

"Do not be a dropout," I told them. "Although I was able to go to college on a ninth-grade education, things have changed. It was difficult for me to try to read and do math problems. Algebra was all I knew; the other forms of math were foreign to me."

I shared with them that I was unable to help my grandchildren with their schoolwork. "What the kids are doing now in the fourth grade is what I was doing in the ninth grade, fifty years ago." This was very embarrassing to me. I told the students the truth and stressed to them how important it was to get an education; to stay in school and take every day seriously.

I wanted them to know that I believed in them. I wanted them to stay in school and not make the same mistake that I made. I focused on their positive characteristics. I told them how it felt being poor, not having sweaters to wear in the cold or shoes to wear on the cold ground; how it felt to not have food to eat or lotion to put on my skin; instead, I had to use the fish grease or lard in the frying pan from supper to wipe the ash from my skin.

I told them that the kids would throw spitballs and trash at my siblings and me as we walked to school in the rain, sleet, or snow.

I also told them that although the other kids made fun of me and my siblings, when they laughed or made fun of me, I would read and pray, read and pray, read and pray.

I feel that my reading and praying paid off. I was able to go to college, complete graduate school, and now own my own businesses. My God is a good God.

I see some of those same kids, adults now, who made fun of me, and they have not made any progress in life.

Treat everyone right. Respect everyone, regardless of the color of their skin or where they come from. You cannot judge people by what they wear, the length of their hair, or the tone of their voices.

It's what's within someone that makes that person who they are. It has to come from within. And most of all, you have to believe in yourself.

After I obtained my master's degree, I furthered my career in nursing and administration.

Chapter 4

Annette: Walk Down Memory Lane

At forty-six years old, I'd been a widow for two years and was the mother of four talented sons. Even though I had a difficult childhood and had dropped out of high school, I was the only child of the eight children in my family who completed college and graduate school.

I had started my career as a registered nurse and worked as an administrator in a local mental health institution.

Times were hard, and I sometimes didn't know where to go or how to get there. I was lonely and depressed. My sons, however, were always there to comfort me, and at times, they saw themselves as my protectors.

One beautiful day, as I sat in my upstairs bedroom, looking out at the beautiful trees in the neighborhood, I heard a voice call to me from under my window. It was my godfather.

He said, "You were on my mind, child. Why are you sitting up there?"

"I'm so tired of being alone, Pop," I said.

"You are a good person," he told me. "You are beautiful, and you have a good heart. Do not worry. The Lord will send you someone— and soon—to take care of you."

God is good; I believe in God. I believe that I am a child of God. I believe that I was placed on this earth with a mission to fulfill.

I have focused on that mission and the mate God appointed for me. He paved the way for us to walk this path together—our destiny.

I was an elected official for the Wilkinson County Board of Education for twelve years. I would travel to Atlanta or Savannah to attend meetings at least twice a year. It was quite ironic and coincidental that I ended up with the same hotel room number, 312, on each occasion but in different locations. I mentioned this to a minister friend, who informed me that this was a sign and that I needed to study it a little harder to search for its meaning. He also said, "Check out your lottery and Cash 3."

The following Monday, I went to a store to buy a lottery ticket. I had no knowledge of how to play a number or what it meant. I didn't even know the cost of a ticket. I just did what he had said. We believe in our ministers, so I figured there must be something to what he'd said.

I entered the store to play this number in the Cash 3 lottery and asked the store clerk for assistance. Before she could help, I heard a pleasant male voice behind me say, "I can help you with that."

I hesitated at first, but then I looked in his eyes, and there was something there—something that I had never seen before.

After he finished helping me, he asked, "What's your name? Are you married? Can I call you? Will you answer the phone when I call?"

Is this my surprise? I wondered. *Is this what those Cash 3 numbers meant?* As it turned out, I didn't hit the lottery that day—or did I? He was my mate, the mate that my godfather had told me the Lord would send me, the mate to whom my minister friend directed me.

Isn't this a mystery? How did this happen?

---— Chapter 5 ———

Annette: The First Date

After meeting Joseph for the first time, when he helped me to work out the Cash3 lottery, I gave him my office phone number, not my personal number. I wasn't entirely sure about this guy, even though he had that look about him, but I looked into his eyes and decided to give him a chance. Normally, I would not have gone that far, but something was there, and I was eager to find out what it was.

He was handsome and clean-cut and had a smile that was out of this world. And his walk was sexy.

As I was leaving the store, I said, "OK, call me around four o'clock. I should be finished with my meetings by then."

I returned to my office, and around two thirty, my secretary informed me that I had a call on the line. "It's a male," she said, "but he wouldn't give his name."

That guy can't tell time, I thought. I refused to answer the call and told my secretary to take a message.

Thirty minutes later, he called back. This time, he left his name—Joe. Again, I refused to answer the phone. Around four o'clock, he called back, and I answered the phone.

"I've been trying to reach you," he said. "I know we agreed to talk around four, but I couldn't wait."

He invited me out to dinner. I accepted, and we went to one of the familiar restaurants in town.

It was an interesting date. He sat across from me and smiled the entire time we were there. I couldn't tell if he was smiling at me or with me or in response to what I was saying—or maybe he just loved to smile.

After I got to know him better, I discovered that his smile was part of his personality—a part that I liked.

During our first date, he gave me a general overview of his life. He made one remarkable comment that has stayed in my memory to this day. He said, "Annette, you are going to hear some things about me. Some are true, but the majority are false. People tend to remember the bad things, stretch them to the limit, and squash the good things." He took my hands and looked into my eyes. "If there is anything that you want to know or have clarified, or if you have any doubt about the accuracy, please talk with me before you make a final decision about me. Please give me a chance to prove who I am and the kind of person I am."

He took a deep breath and then said, "I have done some things in my life, and I have walked some long, dreary roads, but I did not walk them alone. I have always believed that my God was there with me, and when I went in a hole, he brought me out. When I shed a tear, he was there to wipe it away. When I couldn't sleep at night, I would pick up the Bible that I kept beside my bed, and I would read verse after verse until I fell asleep.

"I have done things that I am not proud of, but we are all human and have made mistakes. I believe in God. He is a powerful person, and he has always been there for me."

I looked not only into his eyes but deeply into his soul and his heart, and I thought, *Is this who my godfather and my minister friend were trying to tell me would be here for me? Is this my mate?*

I just wasn't ready to accept that. I could not believe it. Still, there was something about this guy, a feeling that I couldn't shake, something I'd felt on the first day I'd met him—it might have been love at first sight.

Was that it? *Was* this love at first sight or, as a friend suggested, "just lust"?

After that first date, he called every day, sometimes three times a day. I finally agreed to a second date. He took me to a Mexican restaurant, one to which I'd never been.

I thought I was dressed surprisingly well, but let me tell you about him. His waist was smaller than mine, and he had wide shoulders, so he resembled a professional football player. He looked handsome, and his pants really fit him. His smile could wipe me away. Although he didn't know it, and I didn't dare to share it, his smile, profile, and masculinity just made me melt to the floor.

I knew that his primary goal that night was to impress me.

"Order whatever you want," he said. "How about a drink? It's all on me."

I ordered a steak dinner with a margarita, and he ordered the same. We had a ball; the food and drinks were good. We laughed and talked and got to know even more about each other.

We finished eating, and our server brought the check. As he held it in his hand, he looked like he might choke—the expression on his face was one of deep concern. I immediately lowered my head, for I didn't want him to know that I'd noticed his expression.

He cleared his throat and said, "Is this right? What did we order?"

The total bill for our meal was fifty-five dollars; he had only fifty-eight dollars. He not only did not have enough for the tip, but he also didn't have enough for gas and food for the next day. He gave a one-dollar tip and saved the remaining two dollars for the next day.

What an impression he'd made! But through his embarrassment, he held on to that smile.

At the end of the night, he still didn't give up. "When can I see you again?" he asked.

I didn't give an answer right then. I had to absorb what had just happened. I wasn't sure if he could afford to meet my wants and needs. I loved to go out and loved to eat at fancy restaurants.

Joseph phoned me the following day and said, "I'm going to have to find another job that pays more money."

"Why would you leave your current job?" I asked.

"So that I can maintain a woman of your character and status," he answered. "I need to make more money."

After much consideration—and the fact that I could not get rid of those feelings inside me—I concluded that my deep feelings overrode any concern over money. *Having money is not all that makes a relationship,* I told myself.

Chapter 6

Annette: Commitment to a Relationship

Loneliness, staying at home, sitting in the chaise lounge all alone night after night and day after day—it brought my thinking to reality. *Why am I here? Why am I sitting alone? Should I give that young man a try? Should I do a little more research on him?*

I went to my "gossip team"—those friends who had my best interests at heart, or so they said. Some told me about marriage, although they'd never been married. Some told me what to do and what to look out for, although they'd never been in a concrete relationship themselves. Some of them even called me or came to my office or my home to give me a long history of Joseph and his past relationships.

They always had the ugly but nothing good. They shared incidents that had occurred more than twenty years ago. I listened, but even as I did, I could not help but say, "People do change. Are you telling me that this young man has not changed in over twenty years?"

They could not answer.

That wasn't me. I had been through the storm, and I knew when something hurt. I knew what it was to be looked down on and not given an opportunity to breathe or to strive.

The saddest part about this issue was the kids. My children heard so much negative talk about Joseph from the community that they were confused. They would look at me and him, and they would show disapproval about our relationship.

Then, my oldest son phoned me one morning and asked, "Mama, are you happy with Joseph?"

"Yes, son, I am as happy as I have ever been," I answered.

"If you are happy, Mama, I am happy for you," he said. "That's all I wanted to know."

After that conversation, I could see the relief on my other sons' faces, and their attitudes toward Joseph changed tremendously.

After so much negativity, I sat down with my best friend and shared the things that had occurred—the phone calls and my conversation with my oldest son. "Tell me the truth," I said. "You're from Joseph's hometown and know a lot about him and his history."

"He's a good person," she said. "We all make mistakes in our lives. You must turn to God, our almighty Father, and *believe in him*. He will show you the way." She shared with me her own ups and downs and then said, "If you think he is someone you can love, hang on to him. Leave all the gossipers out there because they are not in your relationship. If you want to give him a chance, you do that. Who are they to pass judgment on him? I'm going to keep both of you in my prayers." Then she reached out and held my hand, and we prayed together.

Of all the so-called friends who called and attempted to give me advice, not one of them asked to pray for my and Joseph's relationship or held my hand in prayer.

Together, my best friend and I recited a scripture:

> But I say unto you, love your enemies, bless them that curse you, do well for them that hate you, and pray for them which despitefully use you, and persecute you. (Matthew 5:44)

After deep consideration, I committed to a relationship with Joseph.

---------------- *Chapter 7* ----------------

Joseph: Walk Down Memory Lane

I was born in a small country town in Hancock County, Georgia. I was the second of six siblings, five brothers and one sister. My sister was never alone. We brothers were always there for her. My parents, Roy and Gladys Trawick raised us as a close family. We were always there for each other.

When I was ten years old, my family moved away from Hancock County. My father was a farmer, and my mother was an entrepreneur. She loved children and opened one of the first day care centers in 1970.

Both of my parents were hard workers and provided us with whatever we needed.

On Saturdays, my parents would go to downtown Milledgeville, and we would visit my uncle. I would separate myself from the family and go down the street to talk to the elderly ladies and men who lived there.

One Saturday, I did my usual visiting with the elderly people who lived near my uncle. This day, though, one of the old ladies kept staring at me.

"What are you looking at?" I asked her.

"You have a glow over your head," she said

"What do you mean?"

"You have a glow," she repeated. "That glow indicates that you are a blessed child, and one day, you will be rich—by the age of forty-nine."

"How do you know I'll live to see forty-nine?" I asked.

She simply said, "You will."

I was stunned with disbelief. I immediately ran and told my mom what the older lady had said.

"She might be right," my mom said. "Older people can see things. They can look within your soul and predict the future."

I shared the elderly lady's words with my sister and brothers, but they did not believe me.

As I got older, I realized what she had said, and I can recall some of the things that I experienced in my life. I feel now that what she said might have meaning.

At age fourteen, I started to work at my first job. My parents purchased a car for my brother and me to share; he was fifteen. Neither of us had a driver's license, but we were able to drive back and forth to work and school.

In the 1960s, Pop had another side job—moonshining. To survive and to pay the car note, we had to help Pop with this side job. I was remarkably familiar with the ingredients at the time, but I can't remember them now.

I have talked with my children and have stressed to them the importance of getting a good education and working.

Getting up in the middle of the night to go coon hunting was not fun for me. I learned a lot, but I would not wish that experience on anyone. My pop would read the *Farmer's Almanac*, and when he saw there was going to be a full moon, he told us to get ready. Around one o'clock in the morning, I would hear him outside my window, getting the bloodhounds ready—they would be barking.

Pop would say, "Let's go, Joe." It seemed that I was the only one who went with him most of the time. My other brothers went too, but I felt I went more often than the others.

Down through the woods we went, with the hound dogs running and barking. I ran through the briars and tree limbs and across holes in the ground. I knew I'd better not fall because I'd be left behind, especially if the hounds treed a coon. We had to find our way through the woods without a flashlight; Pop had the only flashlight. The only thing I had was the kerosene lamp and the sack to carry the coon.

I can proudly talk about this memory now, and I realize how thankful I am today, for the Lord has brought me a mighty long way.

When I was a teenager, Friday night was when other guys hung out at the nightclub, but in our house, Friday night was coon hunting night. We would go out on Fridays so that we would have enough food—meat—for Sunday dinner. Survival—I learned this trait from my father. You must work hard to have something in life. He always said, "Hard work never hurt anybody."

During the 1960s, nature provided families with whatever they needed, from food to Christmas trees. Back then, life was what you made of it, and it still is what you make of it now. As of this writing, in 2021, things have changed, but the concept of working for what you need is still a major focus.

I didn't get the chance to go out on Friday nights as much as some people, but I made up for it on Saturday night. My teenage years were typical teenage years—getting into fights, car racing, and chasing girls.

As time passed, I had some growing pains, as everyone did. I had some challenges. I made some good and not-so-good decisions, but I learned from them, and they made me stronger.

I went through some things at age thirty-two and older. I had some hard struggles with life and relationships.

Chapter 8

Joseph: Struggles

I married at age nineteen, purchased a home, and raised four children. I divorced at age thirty-two. This was an exceedingly difficult time for me. The divorce was devastating for me because I did not want it. I was left with the responsibility of sharing my four children, every other weekend. I followed this routine until they became teenagers.

I am so proud of my oldest son. He is retired military, retired from one of the most prestigious air forces in the military, Special Forces. He is married to a beautiful woman, and they have two children and two grandchildren.

My oldest daughter is a registered nurse with a master's degree and presently works as an administrator. She is a proud mom of four children and is soon to be a grandma. We are so proud of our granddaughter who is a certified school teacher.

My second son is a very independent young man and owns his own business. We are proudly waiting on that first grandchild.

My second daughter adds another joy of success to the family. She is an author and licensed insurance agent. She has thrilled our home with three beautiful grandchildren.

I look back over my struggles and can proudly say that all my kids are doing well in life and have careers.

At age thirty-five, times were still hard for me. One night, I was very depressed. My mind told me to get my Bible. I cut off all the lights in the house so that it was dark. I went into the den and turned on one light so I could see. As I opened the Bible and begin to read, I felt very relieved. It was as if all my worries and problems began to fade away.

I stopped reading, looked up, and asked God to help me. As I spoke those words, I felt fresh air come into my body, as if my body was being cleansed. Then I felt a warmth inside of me, as if God was inside me. It felt as if he was saying that he would be with me, wherever I went.

I said, "God, let your will be done."

After that, I felt that whenever I went into a hole, God led me out of it. Whenever I felt hopeless, he gave me hope. Whenever I didn't know how I could pay my bills, he made a way. When my vehicle broke down up, I was provided with a car.

I had a dream a week after that experience. The dream revealed my death at age sixty-four. It was then that I realized I had to turn my life around. I quit drinking, smoking, and running the streets. It was as if my God was driving me in the right direction.

Now, I can understand what the old lady told me when I was six years old—that I had a glow around my head and that I would be rich by the time was I forty-nine. I am now seventy-two years old. Praise to the Lord. She said I would be rich, but *rich* has many definitions, not just regarding money. I know where my richness lies.

I can honestly share that there is a God. He walked with me throughout my struggles. He gave (and continues to give) me insight into my life. I know that whatever you do in life, you have to treat people right, and you will be rewarded. And always honor your mother and father.

When I was struggling, I could have taken the easy way out and turned to drugs, alcohol, and the streets. Instead, I turned to the Lord, and he helped me. He made me stronger when I got knocked down, and I got up. When I was unable to get up, I crawled until I could get up. I refused to stay down.

Life is a strange thing, and life is what you make of it. From the date of your birth, your destiny is already established. It depends on you, however, as to how you reach it. All of your steps will not be successful, and all of your failures will not result in sadness. But do not give up. Keep the Lord in your life, and he will guide you. I believe this because he has guided me. My God is a good God.

You will make mistakes in life that you cannot take back. Do not dwell on those mistakes. They are done; you cannot take them back. We are all human. Move on, move on, and move on.

—— Chapter 9 ——

Joseph: A Mother's Child

My mother worried about me because I was single again at age forty-nine. All of her children were married except my older brother and me.

I went to visit my mother one Mother's Day, and she said, "Isn't it about time for you to get married again?"

"I haven't met the right one yet," I said. "I can't marry someone I don't love, just to say I'm married. I feel that the Lord is going to send me that right person, and when he does, I will know."

My mother replied, "He will send you somebody."

The *right person* is one who wants what you want, someone who says, "Take my hand, and let's go." It's someone who is not afraid to take chances—a daredevil. Someone who is not afraid to step out on faith. Someone who sees life as a challenge and a thrill, a rush of blood through the body, and an experience that will never be forgotten.

The right person is someone who believes in themselves and feels confident that they can do whatever anyone else can do—and do it just as good or better.

Let me tell you: being single was not fun for me. I slept alone many nights and didn't want to be bothered. There also were times, however, when I wanted someone to love, someone next to me. Still, I refused to accept just anyone because I knew that what I wanted was out there, and the Lord eventually would bring that person to me.

My loneliness came during the holidays. Christmas was the most depressing of all—not getting together with the family with my lady at my side; the children split between both parents; not having special dishes—the ham, cakes—or swapping gifts with family members.

The next depressing holiday was Fourth of July. I was with my family, but I didn't have a mate. I occupied my time with being the chef—I did all the cooking.

Let's not forget New Year's Eve—no one to kiss when the New Year comes in; no toast of the New Year's drink, and no special person to take to the New Year's Eve party. I could have had a woman at my side, but I chose not to because she wouldn't have been the right one. And I wouldn't accept just anyone. So I stayed at home.

I knew where I wanted to go and knew I needed to make a journey. I knew that God had that right lady to make that journey with me, so I patiently waited. I believed he would let me know. My God is a good God.

Finding a way to occupy my time was a task. I would go to work every day but dreaded the end of the workday because I had to go home to an empty house. Once I got home, I had to prepare my own meal, unless I went to McDonald's, Dairy Queen, or Burger King for a fast meal. I didn't often go to fast-food places because my budget was so tight. Finding odds and ends in the refrigerator was the best I could do.

I watched TV at night and loved to watch the History Channel. Some stories depicted movie stars and rich people who fell from grace, and that was very interesting. I would ask myself how someone could have so much but then, in the end, have nothing. I promised myself that if I ever got out of the hole I was in, I would never go back.

It was interesting how drugs, alcohol, women, and choosing the wrong path could cause someone to lose everything. I learned a lot from watching the ruin of famous people in history.

History can guide you in the right direction, if you pay close attention to it.

God gave us minds to think and to make good decisions. As I traveled this road of loneliness, I could not forget what I saw and learned on the History Channel.

When I invited Annette to my home, we sat down and watched the History Channel together. I can name movie stars, events in their lives, and the movies they made and the costars of those movies. I shared things about them with Annette, and that made me feel good because I knew something she didn't know. I knew that I had made an impression on her because I watched her out of the corner of my eye and saw a big smile on her face.

I had her attention as well. She would cuddle with me, and I knew that I had scored with the most beautiful and educated woman in the county.

I thought Annette was beautiful, smart, and a trailblazer. I was afraid someone would steal her away from me. What a smile she had. She wore her hair short on the side and long on top, and it was always in place and beautiful.

I loved to see her walk; she had those big pretty legs. She walked with distinction. No one else walked like that, only her. Her perfume was soft and sweet, a scent that I could smell all night and enjoy every moment.

I stopped smoking at age forty. I used to smoke ten cigars a day—as if they were going out of style, or I was going to get a prize for smoking the most.

One day, I watched a History Channel program that talked about a movie star who had died from lung cancer, and they showed how his lungs looked after death. He had been a heavy smoker, up to two packs of cigarettes a day. He had been smoking since age thirteen.

Right then, I took the cigar I was smoking, broke it in half, and placed it in a glass of water. After two hours, the water was brown, and I couldn't see through it. It was the same color as the pictures of the cancerous lungs that I'd seen on History Channel.

I promised myself that I would not smoke another cigar, and to this day, I have not. On my last chest x-ray, thirty years ago, my attending physician informed me that I was lucky that I had stopped smoking when I did because he still could see scar formation from the smoke in my lungs.

Being home alone can bring about a lot of things. I did things that I normally would not have done if I'd had someone there with me to maybe guide or look after me.

I was a closet drinker—at home, drinking by myself, and nobody knew but me. When I was in public, I often frowned on others who drank. If the truth was only known, my favorite drink was beer and apple cider wine. I would drink it whenever it was available. When I was with my friends and relatives on weekends, holidays, or special occasions, we would drink three or four cases of beer. I did it so long, until I got tired of it.

The History Channel and Annette changed my perception of drinking. One night, I was home alone and had several bottles of wine available to me. Annette came home, and I yelled at her and frightened her. She said she had seen something in my eyes that had her too afraid to move.

Right then, she sat me down and told me, "Something has to go— either the wine or me."

I knew that I could not bear to lose her, so I stopped drinking, right then and there. That is living proof that a habit can be broken. If there is something in your life that you want badly enough, you can stop a bad habit if you want to.

I had been single for twenty-three years, and it was the most unhappy and miserable time of my life. I was lonely, and I was tired of being with different people I really didn't want to be with. I felt that I had met the right person, and I wasn't going to let anything interfere with that. When Annette told me that I had frightened her, and she gave me the choice of her or alcohol, I knew what I had to do. I let the alcohol go. No way was I going back to where I had been. The Lord sent her to me, and I was not going to let anybody or anything come between us.

There is a difference between lust and love. When you meet the right person, your heart will let you know. You won't let anything interfere with that.

Chapter 10 ——————

The Wedding

Joseph

My mom always worried that I wouldn't meet anyone, and now that I felt that I had found her, I was eager for my mother and father to meet her.

When we reached the house, I said, "Mom, this is my friend Annette. I brought her to meet you."

I could not wait to see the look in my mother's eyes. She and I had a special relationship. I knew when my mom approved—or disapproved—of something I was doing. When I introduced Annette to her, her eyes brightened, and she gave me that nod. I knew then I had scored. I could see relief on her face.

My dad was a little bit different. He was always on the go and could not sit in a chair for five minutes without doing something. But this time, he sat down with us, and he and Annette had a very good conversation. They talked about family history and work. They had something in common, and that was hard work. Her godfather and my dad hit it off right away. They both liked dressing up in stylish suits, neckties, and shoes.

Later in the conversation, my dad asked me when we were getting married. He wanted me to get married right away. I think he was afraid that I would lose her if we waited. Little did he know that I held a close grip on her and had no intention of letting her go.

My parents farmed and had many yard animals. I was proud to show off all the farm animals and fresh vegetables. Annette enjoyed this and talked about when she was growing up and how her parents would plant collard greens, peas, and corn in the backyard. She even helped me feed the hogs and chickens. I had found someone who loved to work and did not mind getting dirty.

As she became more comfortable with my parents, she would help Dad pick peas and butter beans. I wasn't very interested in working in the fields, so I stayed away from that as much as I could.

My dad grew watermelons too, and Annette loved watermelons. Going out into the field to pull her a big juicy one was special to me. I loved to see that smile on her face. My dad liked Annette and would get upset when I would visit them without her. For my dad to like her, I knew we had something special. Also, my mom would smile when she saw us together. I knew I had hit the jackpot, and that was one of the things that the old lady had talked about when she said I was going to be rich.

I realized that being rich was not all about money. It was finding the right mate—to feel loved and to be loved; to be happy when you feel sad; to laugh when things are not humorous; to smile when you are in pain; and to be able to help someone when they need help.

I was happy with Annette, but I wondered if she felt the same way about me. I felt like a million dollars when I was with her. We went places that were new to me. We traveled out of town and to other states—six hundred or eight hundred miles was nothing to us. We would just ride, ride, and ride. As long as we were together, we were happy.

The time came for us to get serious; we decided to get married. None of the kids were happy to hear this at first, but they wanted whatever we wanted to make us happy. They were attacked by the community gossipers, who told them why we should not marry. But as time went on, they appeared to be as happy as we were.

Everyone in our pasts had something to say about us getting married, but no one had anything concrete to justify their negative comments. Annette and I knew what we wanted, and we knew that if we wanted our marriage to work, we had to build a shield around us and our kids. We closed people out of our circle and were very careful who we allowed into it.

One morning, Annette and I were lying in bed when the phone rang. A female voice on the other end of the phone identified herself as one of Annette's cousins. I gave Annette the phone, and her cousin began to tell Annette why she should not marry me—I could hear her because Annette was lying in my arms. The cousin told her about something that had happened in my life thirty years earlier, and she compared me to her ex-husband. She then said that she was calling on behalf of some family members.

After a lengthy conversation, Annette ended the phone call by saying, "I love Joseph, and if there is anything I need to know about him, I will find out about it myself. Our wedding will be December 16. Thanks for the information. I'll send you an invitation to the wedding."

We didn't hear from that cousin again, and we decided we didn't want her at the wedding.

Annette

The most exciting part about the wedding plans was breaking the good news to Joseph's father and my godfather. They both were old-fashioned and as old as Joseph. My godfather said Joseph had to ask him for my hand in marriage. Can you imagine, a fifty-year-old woman getting permission to get married? That was a joke.

We shared the good news with Mr. and Mrs. Trawick, Joseph's father and mother. This was in April, and we told them we had set a wedding date of December 16. Mr. Trawick rose up in his chair, looked at me, and loudly asked, "Why are you waiting so long? That's a long way off."

His mother just smiled and nodded her head. We knew that we had her approval. Getting his mother's approval meant so much to Joseph.

What a day it was on December 16. We had four hundred guests. We hadn't realized so many people were interested in our wedding. We received so many gifts. We had enough cash in gifts to pay for our honeymoon cruise and expenses to the Bahamas.

Our wedding party consisted of twenty-five bridesmaids and twenty-five groomsmen. We were so happy. We both had been married previously, but neither one of us had had a church wedding, so we went all the way.

Tradition dictates that a virgin or a woman who has never been married should wear a white gown. I was neither, but I wore a white gown anyway—this was my wedding, and I did not care what anyone thought. I didn't believe in tradition. I hadn't had the opportunity the first time to get married in a white dress, so I did when I married Joseph. I believe in doing what you want to do and how you want to do it, as long as you are not hurting anyone.

After the wedding and returning home from the honeymoon, our future plans as a family began.

Our wedding

---------------------------- *Chapter 11* ----------------------------

Establishing Businesses

Annette

Joseph drove trucks and I worked as a nurse administrator. Joseph would come home, complaining about his job; he refused to do things not assigned in his job description.

One day, I told him, "It appears that you need to work for yourself."

So we set out to find something that did not require many skills or much knowledge. His first business, in 2001, was establishing a cleaning service. We called it Trawick Professional Cleaning Services. We advertised and landed several small jobs here and there. The first job was stripping and waxing floors at commercial stores. Joseph did not know anything about stripping and waxing floors, so he hired someone with experience who was able to do the job. unfortunately, he didn't know that this person was undependable. He had to postpone several jobs because the worker didn't show up, and Joseph couldn't do the job. He decided that he needed to learn this skill. He paid the employee to show him how to operate the buffer and stripper machines and trained himself for three consecutive days, with the worker looking on. After the third day, Joseph no longer needed the worker because he had mastered that skill.

A good rule of thumb is to make sure you can perform the jobs or have the skills for whatever business you operate. Never depend on someone else. You need to be in a position to do whatever your employees do or whatever the job requires. To better promote your business, make sure you are performing the best that you can do. We believe in 100 percent proficiency.

One day, we received a phone call about cleaning newly built condos. We accepted the job, even though we had never done a condo cleanup. We tackled the job and were successful. This was a learning experience for us as well.

Joseph

I had Trawick Professional Cleaning Services going, and Annette was getting Ratliff Private Home Care off the ground. We sat down and discussed both businesses. We know we would need to fall back on one of them if the other business slowed down. This was a good strategy, which paid off in the end.

During 2011, Annette started a CNA (certified nursing assistant) training program. This was something that she had worked on for several years before we married. One day, we were sitting at the dinner table, and I asked her what she had done with the training program she had worked on.

She went into the closet, pulled it off the shelf, and went back to completing it, after much encouragement from me. Now the program is one of the most successful programs in the state of Georgia.

In 2015, Annette landed a contract with the State of Georgia to supply CNAs to a nearby hospital. This contract lasted for four years and was one of the most productive contracts for both of us. We worked together, hand in hand, and made this contract a success.

In 2016, Global Transit, LLC, was established and remains in operation today.

—— *Chapter 12* ——

Where Are We Today?

Annette

It has been a long journey for Joseph and me. We reflect on how we got started and where we are today. We also think about the old woman who told Joseph. "One day, you will be rich." After fifty years of struggles, I now can proudly say, yes, we are rich.

Joseph

Annette and I are still happily married. We stepped into some holes in the road, and the Lord led us out. We believed in each other and believed in ourselves. We felt there was nothing that we could not do. We felt that no one was better than us.

We fell down on many occasions, but we raised up and started again. We have cried together and wiped our eyes many times, and we have prayed together.

We refused to accept failure.

Annette and Joseph

As a married couple, we knew that we had to stick together and not let the devil in. We knew that the devil comes in many shapes and fashions. A lot of times, the devil tries to come into your home through your children, friends, or family.

As entrepreneurs, you need to guard your business and not let anyone take it from you or jeopardize it. They will come in as your friends and attempt to steal your ideas and trade. Just remember, building your business is like building your house. You will know where every brick is.

Thieves will not be able to grow from your success, but they will try.

Whatever you do in your business, do it 100 percent; be the best at what you do.

Sometimes in life, you may feel like a duck in a pond. You see the duck sitting on the water, and it seems as if it's not moving, but underneath the water, that duck is paddling steadily. You look again, and that duck is on the other side of the pond. How did it get there? That's the secret to life—be like the duck; never stop paddling. Keep going, and you will reach your destination. We did!

Love your mate. It's not all good every day. You will have bad days and good days. Believe in yourself and in God, and he will lead you.

We are all human, and we all make mistakes. Do not dwell on those mistakes. Find something positive in the mistake, and make good of it. You can't change what happened yesterday, but you can make a better path going forward from what you learned.

Riches come in all shapes and fashions. We are rich in the following ways:

➢ We believe in the Lord, and praise him every day.

➢ We don't have much money, but we have each other.

➢ We have love for each other, and we love each other.

➢ We have children we love, and they are productive and have careers, and that's from what we taught them along the way.

➢ We have grandchildren, friends, and families.

➢ We are healthy; we can walk, talk, and find our way. When one of us needs help, the other is there to help.

➢ We are entrepreneurs. The Lord showed us the way so that we could pursue our dreams and goals.

➢ We have a home (shelter) and feel safe every day.

➢ Our God is a good God, and he has never failed us. We will always praise and honor him.

As mentioned earlier, we traveled our path from rags to riches. Some people assume that being rich refers to having money and material things and that rags refers to being without the best; being poor, shameful, and needy.

We saw *rags* and being poor as a positive thing. It helped us to grow, to be strong, and to help us find our way.

Being poor and not having what we thought we should have, like others, helped us to accept the Lord as our mighty Savior. God made us all, and he gave us all common sense and the ability to be productive.

We believe that it is within all of us to take what the Lord has given us and turn it into what we want it to be. Whether it's reaching a goal in life, finding the right mate or the right job, or doing the work for the Lord.

You need faith and belief in yourself. You also have to believe in the Lord, our mighty Savior and follow his footsteps.

There will be times when you may find yourself in a hole but then certainly find yourself coming out of that hole. To whom do you give praise?

We know to whom to give praise. It was the work of the Lord, and we praise him *every day*.

If you do not have God in your life, we challenge you to search your soul and heart for him, to walk in faith, and to surrender to God to produce miracles in your life. This is one of the riches that we cherish and a blessing that got us where we are today.

We know that some individuals are traveling the same road that we traveled fifty years ago—the road of distress, self-pity, shame, and disbelief. Do not do that. Stop right now, and take a look at yourself and where you are today.

Ask yourself:

➤ Do I want to do better?

➤ Is this where I want to be in life?

➤ Is this my dream or goal?

➤ Where is God in my life?

➤ Do I believe I can do better?

➤ Did I choose the right mate/partner to help me make those major decisions?

➤ Am I afraid to step out and make that move?

It is your decision and your move. Now it is time to do some soul-searching.

What about prayer? Talk to God. He will hear you and help you to make those final decisions. You must believe in him and in yourself. Do you believe?

We ask you again: where are you? Are you where you want to be in life? Do you want to do better?

If you are content with where you are in life and feel that you have reached your potential, then you will not go any farther. But if you feel that you have not reached your potential and want to do better in life, the road is yours to travel.

Hold your head up, keep your eyes on what you want, and go for it. Do not let anyone tell you what you can or cannot do.

Believing in yourself is another one of those riches that we have held so dearly in our hearts. We believe in one another, and we never let anyone tell us what we can or cannot do. We believe in the Lord—and what a wonderful feeling and friend to have.

Wanting to do better for oneself is part of your riches. Have you taken the time to ask yourself where you want to be in life? Are you there yet?

It's not a difficult question.

Think about how you can turn those rags into riches. If you are not where you want to be, and you want to turn those rags into riches, it's never too late to start.

First, given honor to our heavenly Father, who should be the first person in our lives. We need to remember this scripture:

> When thou prays enter into thy closet, and when thy
> hast shut thy door, pray to thy Father which is in secret:
> and thy Father which seethe in secret shall reward thee
> openly. (Matthew 6:6)

---------- *Chapter 13* ----------

What Is Your Goal?

Have you looked at your surroundings? Is this where you want to be? Has your dream become a reality? Did you make it there? If you didn't make it there, ask yourself why.

Let's not make excuses. What is your goal—to be what, to do what, or to be where?

If you had a goal, and you reached that goal, congratulations to you. Thank God, our heavenly Father, for being there and walking those steps with you.

If you did not reach your goal, let's figure out why. This will be the rags, not reaching that goal that you wanted—the shame, self-pity, and anger.

Let's say you don't have what you want out of life. Your friends are doing much better than you are. They have fine homes, cars, clothing, and other material things. They have a good education and are very respected in the community. You wish that you were like them. You wonder how they did it when you could not. You see them going to church on Sunday. When you talk with them, they mention that they feel blessed. Being blessed is what we call *riches*.

Now, what about you?

Did you stay focused? Did you stay in school? Did you believe that you could do what anybody else could do, if you only believed? Did you turn to God and ask him for his help?

When things were hard and you felt that you could not make it another day, what did you do? Did you pray? Did you take an inventory of your life? In taking that inventory, did you see something that you could change and make better? Did you make that change or put it off for another day?

What about mistakes? Did you dwell on them, or did you look on the positive side and figure out ways to avoid making that mistake again, as well as learning from that mistake, to make things better? Did you put what you learned into action to make sure that mistake didn't occur again?

You know where you want to go and when you want to do it. Are you afraid to step out there? Have you ever heard of stepping out on faith? Try it; we did, and it worked for us. You will never know what you can do until you try. Faith is one of our riches that we learned and grew to love as we traveled our path from rags to riches.

Just remember, you do not need money to be rich. Riches are all of those other things that God has blessed you with.

— Chapter 14 —

Where Is God in Your Life?

Every word of God is pure; he is a shield unto them that put their trust in Him.

—Proverbs 30:5

When we are troubled and don't know which way to go, we turn to God. We know that he has led us out of many holes. We know that he has walked along with us, all the way and all the time. We believe in the Lord, and we know that he loves us. If he didn't, we wouldn't be here today to share this book with you.

We need to have faith within, and we have to believe. We can talk all day about having faith, but if you do not believe, then faith will not deliver. It's all within you.

Do some soul-searching and find your way in God's life. That is something you and God will have to work on together.

Joseph

Did you choose the right mate or partner? Have you asked yourself what choosing the right mate or partner has to do with your success in life?

It depends on what your mate means to you. What is their purpose? Are they with you just to say yes or no when you want them to? Is your mate there to help you make major decisions in your life, and vice versa?

Having the right mate is another form of riches. We all have strong and weak characteristics. We know that we are not perfect, and sometimes we need a push, a shove, a prayer, or words of encouragement and sometimes just someone to tell us we are wrong or right.

Sometimes, we need someone to walk with us, someone who wants the same thing out of life that we want; someone who is willing to stand along with us and fight for a common purpose together.

Annette and I have found that in each other, and we feel this is one of the reasons why we have been so successful in our journey from rags to riches.

If you love each other and care for each other, that bond will come. If you do not care for each other, then you will see unrest and struggles.

Annette and I love each other and have loved each other from the first day we met. We call it love at first sight.

My friends called it lust, but what did they know? We are still together, and they are still struggling.

As Mr. Roy Trawick Sr. stated many times, "What God put together, no man or beast can separate."

We cherish that comment today. When times get hard and the devil continues to try to push our door down, we grip each other's hand, pray, and we say that comment over and over again.

This is what we mean about finding the right mate—that person who will stick with you through good and ugly.

A good mate will be with you to the end. When there is a need, a good mate will reach out and help you along.

We fall together; we win together.

If you have no mate, and there is something that you want to do, don't hesitate. Believe in yourself and step out on faith. Remember that you are never alone. God is always with you and will lead the way. Do not give up.

We can also look at a mate as similar to a branch of the military. There are four branches in the US military. When one branch needs help, the others come to the rescue.

Chapter 15 ―――――――

€ntrepreneurs

Is owning your own business a goal or dream in your life? If so, what have you done about it? Did you reach out to fulfill that dream, or did you give up?

We want to share another of our riches with you. When we first started this book, we shared about our businesses and how we got started, but we didn't share the rags and riches that came along with starting those businesses.

God is good, and as we mentioned earlier, you have to believe in yourself. You have to take chances and delay fears. You need a good mate, someone who believe in what you believe in and is willing to go that extra mile.

You have to reach out to each other and communicate. Keep an open line of communication every day.

There is another thing about love with your mate. When one is hurt, the other hurts. You can feel your mate's pain. You can read your mate's mind. When they are thinking, you can hear what they are thinking, as if your mate was speaking out loud.

Starting these businesses was trial and error. We did not know if we would be successful, but we knew it was something we wanted to do, and the only way to find out if we could do it was to try.

There were times when we did not know if we could pay our bills or make payroll for the employees, but it all came through for us. In thirty years of owning our own business, we never missed a payday for our employees. We never missed a utility bill or maintenance fee. We had each other and the Lord.

When one of us was unable to fulfill a need or meet financial obligations, the other partner came through. This is why it's important to have the right mate. You don't need someone who will flee when the times get hot or leave you with all the responsibilities.

You need someone who will stand beside you and with you, through the good and the bad.

Throughout our struggles, many people said to us, "I want to be just like you." Be aware of such a statement, and take it for what it's worth.

What did they mean? Did they want to be like us, or did they want to take what we had built?

They never asked us to sit down with them to show them or help them to be successful. They wanted the easy way out. They wanted to use our brains and our hard work to build an empire for themselves.

When we speak of wanting to help them build their empire, we don't hesitate to share our expertise with anyone. But what we dislike is someone coming in to steal. Be aware of those individuals. They will come in as your friend, but do not allow them to weaken you. You will know and recognize them when you see them.

Remember that building a business is like building a house. You built that house, and you know where every brick lies. It's the same for your business; you built it, so you know how to tear it down. Don't let anyone else tear it down for you. Temptation and jealousy are detrimental to anyone's health and welfare.

Your strength lies within you to be an effective entrepreneur.

When you build a business, build it so strong that when the storm comes, it will be able to withstand the weather.

The "duck theory" has guided us through our journey. Remember: *The key to a successful career is to stay calm on top and to paddle like hell underneath.*

About the Authors

Annette Trawick is a registered nurse and a clinical nurse specialist. She earned her master's degree with a clinical focus in gerontology. She is an entrepreneur and the owner of Collaborative Health Care CNA training program, which holds a five-star rating, and Ratliff Private Home Care.

Joseph Trawick is a high school graduate. He has worked in many fields of industry and always wanted to own his own business. He has twenty-five years' experience as an over-the-road truck driver. He is an entrepreneur, the owner of Trawick Cleaning and Maintenance Services and Global Transit, LLC.

Joseph and Annette have said, "Our greatest accomplishments today are our love for the Lord, our businesses, our children's success, and our marriage."

Printed in the United States
by Baker & Taylor Publisher Services